GW01080134

Elizabeth Bay and the city from Darling Point.

Sydney Opera House

Designed by Jorn Utzon, this unique building took 14 years to build at a cost of $102 million and is a premier attraction visited by millions of tourists every year.
Below: Opening Day — 20th October 1973.
Opposite: The Concert Hall features performances from many world famous artists.

Pier One
One of Sydney's oldest shipping terminals, Pier One has been remodelled to become a major harbourside attraction. It features restaurants, specialty shops, galleries, amusements and strolling musicians.

The Rocks

This compact area on Sydney Cove is the birthplace of Sydney. Now carefully restored, it is full of fascinating relics and buildings of the city's past. Above: Campbell's Store-house (1821) is still partly in use as warehouses, but is now also occupied by restaurants, shops and wine bars. Below: Cadman's Cottage (1816) Sydney's oldest dwelling. Built for the Governor's boat crew and occupied by John Cadman, it is now a maritime musuem.

Above left: The Argyle Centre (1823) in Argyle Street, the main thoroughfare of the Rocks. Hewn from solid rock, the Argyle Cut was started by convicts using hand tools and completed by free labour. Above right: The Hero of Waterloo, one of Sydney's oldest pubs. Below: The towers of modern Sydney dwarf the historic Rocks area.

Above: Argyle Place (1830). A group of early colonial cottages and terraces named by Governor Macquarie after his birthplace Argyle in Scotland. Below: The Garrison Church (1840's). Built of hand-hewn sandstone, this church still serves the local community with regular services.

Sydney Tower

This 305m tower of the Centrepoint complex is the tallest building in Australia and is a focal point for city business and retail trade. Completed in 1981, the slim nine-storey building has shopping complexes, office blocks, convention centres, restaurants and observation decks. The turret at the top of the slender stem has nine levels, four open to the public, with magnificent 360° panoramas away to the horizon 70km distant.

Aerial view of Hyde Park and Sydney Tower.

Hyde Park Barracks (1819)

This elegant Georgian building of sandstone bricks was built to house Sydney's convicts. It has been impressively restored to become the only museum of social history in New South Wales, covering colonial days to the 1950's.

Downtown Sydney

Above: Centrepoint on the corner of Market and Castlereagh Streets is a major shopping complex reflecting the variety of retail shops to be found in the city centre. Below: Martin Place — a popular meeting place with an amphitheatre for lunch-time entertainment.

Queen Victoria Building

Built late last century to house the fruit and vegetable market, this building, occupies an entire city block. Unused for decades, it was re-opened in November 1986. This unique retail complex features beautiful stained glass wheel-arched windows, wrought iron balustrades, a timber shop front and a cathedral stained glass inner dome, all of which recapture the beauty of the Victorian era.

Historical Sydney
Above: Government House (1838) set in magnificent grounds adjoining the Royal Botanical Gardens. Below: St. Mary's Cathedral (1868). The Gothic Style highlights the beautiful qualities of Sydney sandstone.

Above: Elizabeth Farm. Built at Parramatta by John Macarthur in 1793 it is Australia's oldest house. Below: Vaucluse House. This stately residence was the home of W. C. Wentworth — best known for his participation in the exploration of the Blue Mountains and drafting of the Australian Constitution.

Bondi — Australia's most famous beach.

Photo: S. T. Yiap

Looking and Learning

Above: The classic portico of the Art Gallery of New South Wales leads to a vast collection of works by Australian and international artists from all periods. Below: The State Library's Macquarie Street building was opened by Her Majesty the Queen in May 1988.

Photo: Deborah Gillespie — courtesy the State Library of New South Wales

The Royal Botanical Gardens. This is where the first settlers grew their vegetables. Today the gardens feature a pyramid shaped herbarium and an excellent collection of trees, shrubs and flower beds. Below: The Australian Museum houses an extensive exhibition of natural history including this pre-historic Marsupial Lion (Thylacoleo Carnifex).

Photo: Anthony Farr — courtesy the Australian Museum

Sydney Opera House at dusk.

Sydney Nightlife
Kings Cross, famous for its nightclubs and bars, is crowned by the beautiful El Alamein Fountain. Below: The Sydney Entertainment Centre is the largest indoor venue in Australia with a constant procession of concerts, sports and extravaganzas.

Dixon Street. Sydney's Chinatown is lined with restaurants and shops forming a focal point for the Chinese community. Below: When Sydney celebrates it does so with a bang! The harbour makes a spectacular venue for firework displays.

Sydney Harbour
Port Jackson has been claimed as the world's most beautiful deep water harbour and has a shoreline of 244km covering an area of 54 sq. km. Dotted with magnificent beaches, it is internationally renowned for its excellent sailing conditions and facilities, offering equal opportunities to professionals and amateurs alike. The Harbour also makes a glorious setting for the start of the famous Sydney to Hobart "Blue Water Classic" on Boxing Day and the amazing sight of the Ferry Boat Race held every January as part of the Sydney Festival. Pictured: Aerial view of Watson's Bay on the south eastern shores of the harbour. The area is particularly well known for its restaurants and the Watson's Bay Hotel is one of Sydney's more famous watering holes.

Darling Harbour

Originally called Cockle Bay for the abundant shellfish found by the first settlers, Governor Darling gave the harbour its current name in 1826. The harbour remained Australia's busiest port until the 1960's. In 1984 the State Government announced re-development plans, the result of which we see today. Below: Transparent underwater walkways give visitors a rare view of marine life at the Sydney Aquarium.

Above: The Harbourside Festival Market place with its distinctive arched roofline has become the hub of Darling Harbour, combining vast cosmopolitan shopping and eating facilities in an artistic and entertaining environment. Below: Tumbalong Park is named from the original Aboriginal word for the area and is backed by the Exhibition Centre, whose award-winning design of an externally supported roof allows maximum usable space inside.

Above: Aerial view showing the enormous scale of this great re-development, from the Sydney Aquarium and Maritime Museum at the bottom of the picture up to Tumbalong Park and the Entertainment Centre upper left. Below: With a 32 metre wingspan, the Catalina Flying Boat is the largest item on show at the Powerhouse — a collection of science, technology, decorative arts and social history objects.

Above: The Garden of Friendship is a joint venture between the Chinese province of Guangdong and New South Wales and marks the friendship and co-operation between these two sister states. Below: The 3.6 km route of the Harbour Link Monorail joins Darling Harbour to the city centre, enabling quiet, quick and scenic travel for visitors.

Manly A holiday destination in its own right. Above: The Corso, a bustling and colourful thoroughfare linking the ocean and harbour beaches. Below: The line of Norfolk Island Pines give the ocean foreshore a special atmosphere. Opposite: Manly is the first in the long series of Northern beaches that stretch to the mouth of the Hawkesbury River.

The giraffe is the tallest of all living mammals, the long neck being an asset for browsing on leaves and the bark of trees. The female gives birth to a single young every two years. Opposite: Overlooking Taronga Zoo towards the city square.

Taronga Zoo

The name Taronga is an adaptation of an aboriginal word meaning "water view" and the wildlife at Taronga Zoo certainly have a millionaire's outlook of the harbour and the city from the zoo's magnificent setting of 30 hectares of natural bushland and beautiful gardens on the northern shores of the harbour at Mosman.

Recognised as one of the best zoo's in the world, every endeavour has been made to reproduce natural environments for the animals so that people do not intrude and it has a complete collection of Australian wildlife with many species being supplied to zoos around the world.

The nocturnal house provides fascinating glimpses of some of the smaller native mammals that are rarely seen in daylight. The zoo also boasts a spectacular rainforest aviary, a platypus enclosure, aquarium, friendship farm, the popular chimpanzee park and regular acrobatic displays by Australian fur seals.

Right: The Chimpanzee is the most intelligent of all the primates and this reveals itself in many ways including their ability to use tools for specific tasks.

A Kangaroo family — the female in the foreground carrying the young "Joey" in her pouch. Below: Of Australia's many species of parrots, these Rainbow Lorikeets are one of the most colourful.

Australian Wildlife

Geographic isolation of this island continent for millions of years and the diversity of our climate have produced in many instances, animals and birds that are unique in the world.

Over half of Australia's mammals are marsupial. The world's only egg-laying mammals, the Echidna and Platypus are both found here along with the appealing Koala — often mistaken for a bear. One of the most attractive and best known of all Australia's animals, koalas feed exclusively on the young leaves of certain species of eucalypt.

Kangaroos, famous for carrying their young in a pouch, are the world's largest living marsupial. Often up to 2 metres tall they have a remarkable hopping action and using their strong thick tails as a balance can travel steadily at 40km per hour.

There are over 700 species of birds, many native to this country. Of the brilliantly coloured parrots, the Sulphur-crested Cockatoo and the Budgerigar are greatly prized as pets. The flightless Emu is the world's second largest bird capable of running at a speed of 60km per hour and the Lyrebird is renowned for its astonishing prowess as a mimic with an incredible repertoire of calls.

Australia's lovable Koala

Legend of the Three Sisters Once upon a time, three beautiful sisters called Meehni, Wimlah and Gunnedoo lived in the Jamison Valley. The three girls were in love with three brothers from the Dharuk tribe, but their marriage was forbidden by tribal law. The brothers were brave warriors and decided to fight for the girls. During the great battle which followed, the witchdoctor of the girls' tribe turned the sisters to stone. Unfortunately the witchdoctor was killed during the battle, and to this day no one has been able to turn the Three Sisters back into girls.

Around Sydney

Above: The historic Zig Zag railway crossing one of the original sandstone viaducts. Opposite: The Three Sisters, one of many spectacular formations in the Blue Mountains — only a short drive from Sydney. Below: The imposing Devil's Coach House entrance to Jenolan Caves discovered in 1838 by bushranger James McKeown.

Above: The Gap — South Head. Spectacular scenery and one of the best viewing spots for the start of the Sydney to Hobart race. Below: Stanwell Park — a south coast beach close to Wollongong and famous for hang gliding. Opposite: Magnificent Wentworth Falls and the rugged escarpment of Jamison Valley.

Above: Bowral, where the Tulip Time Festival is held in October. Below: Prize Merino rams of today. Australia's wool industry started in the Camden area in the 1790's when John Macarthur imported sheep from India and South Africa. Opposite: Royal National Park, dedicated in 1879, was the first of Australia's National Parks and second in the world. Rugged sea cliffs, waterfalls, rainforests, swamps and woodlands are all in this beautiful area.

Above: Church Point — one of many marinas on The Pittwater. Below: Oyster farming on the Hawkesbury River.

The banks of the Hawkesbury saw some of the Colony's earliest rural development. Today it is better known as a haven for water skiing, fishing and cruising.

Above: Akuna Bay situated in the Ku-Ring-Gai Chase National Park is one of the better known marinas in Australia containing millions of dollars worth of craft. Below: Old Sydney Town. A massive re-creation of Sydney Cove as it was in the 1800's complete with a cast of landed gentry, soldiers, wenches and convicts of those early days.

QANTAS
HILTON
NZI
GOLD FIELDS
Australian
Eagle
SENTRY
SHARP
Bradfield Highway

The city from Lavender Bay.